C000153999

HELEN EXLEY GIFTBOOKS
thoughtful giving starts here...

Published simultaneously in 2001 by Exley Publications Ltd
in Great Britain, and Exley Publications LLC in the USA.

2 4 6 8 10 12 11 9 7 5 3 1

Copyright © Helen Exley 2001
The moral right of the author has been asserted.

ISBN 1-86187-301-8

A copy of the CIP data is available from the British Library on request. All rights
reserved. No part of this publication may be reproduced or transmitted in any
form or by any means, without permission in writing from the publisher.

Edited by Helen Exley.
Illustrated by Juliette Clarke.
Printed in China.

Exley Publications Ltd,
16 Chalk Hill, Watford, Herts WD19 4BG, UK.
Exley Publications LLC,
232 Madison Avenue, Suite 1409, NY 10016, USA.
www.helenexleygiftbooks.com

A SPECIAL GIFT OF
WISDOM

Illustrated by Juliette Clarke

A HELEN EXLEY GIFTBOOK

EXLEY
NEW YORK • WATFORD, UK

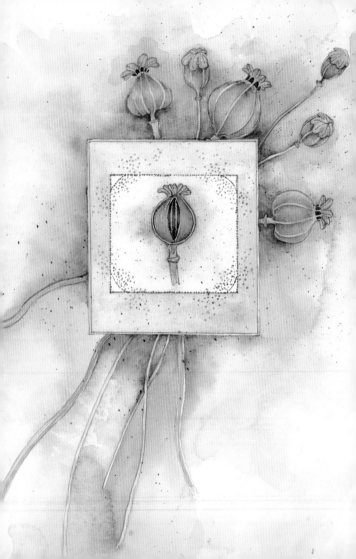

LIFE DIRECTIONS

The first step to wisdom is to be sure
one says and does what one believes.

PAM BROWN, B.1928

–

Indifference is the invincible giant
of the world.

OUIDA

–

If I lose my direction, I have to look for
the North Star, and I go to the north.
That does not mean that I expect to arrive
at the North Star. I just want to go in that
direction.

THICH NHAT HANH

–

If we are facing in the right direction,
all we have to do is to keep on walking.

ANCIENT BUDDHIST EXPRESSION

–

Find the journey's end in every step.

RALPH WALDO EMERSON (1803-1882)

LIFE'S TRUE WEALTH

The wisdom of life consists in
the elimination of nonessentials.

LIN YUTANG (1895-1976)

—

He knew how to be poor without the least
hint of squalor or inelegance.... He chose
to be rich by making his wants few.

RALPH WALDO EMERSON (1803-1882),
ABOUT HENRY DAVID THOREAU

—

I live in a very small house but my windows
look out on a very large world.

CONFUCIUS (551-479 B.C.)

—

And now that I don't want to own anything
any more and am free, now I suddenly own
everything, now my inner riches are
immeasurable.

ETTY HILLESUM (1914-1943)

—

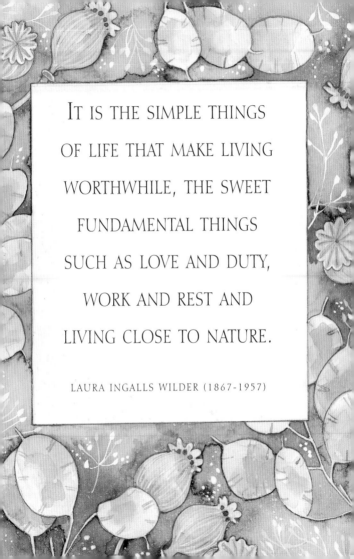

IT IS THE SIMPLE THINGS
OF LIFE THAT MAKE LIVING
WORTHWHILE, THE SWEET
FUNDAMENTAL THINGS
SUCH AS LOVE AND DUTY,
WORK AND REST AND
LIVING CLOSE TO NATURE.

LAURA INGALLS WILDER (1867-1957)

LIVE LIFE FULLY!

The most evident token and apparent
sign of true wisdom is a constant and
unconstrained rejoicing.

MICHEL DE MONTAIGNE (1533-1592)

–

To fill the hour – that is happiness; to fill
the hour, and leave no crevice for a
repentance or an approval.

RALPH WALDO EMERSON (1803-1882)

–

Is not life a hundred times too short
for us to bore ourselves?

FRIEDRICH WILHELM NIETZSCHE (1844-1900)

–

We are all in the gutter,
but some of us are looking at the stars.

OSCAR WILDE (1854-1900)

–

Who is narrow of vision cannot be
big-hearted; who is narrow of spirit cannot
take long, easy strides.

CHINESE PROVERB

–

If you can walk you can dance.
If you can talk you can sing.

ZIMBABWEAN PROVERB

–

I finally figured out the only reason
to be alive
is to enjoy it.

RITA MAE BROWN, B.1944

–

BOUND TO BE TRUE TO YOURSELF

I AM NOT BOUND TO WIN
BUT I AM BOUND TO BE TRUE.
I AM NOT BOUND TO SUCCEED
BUT I AM BOUND TO LIVE UP TO
WHAT LIGHT I HAVE.

ABRAHAM LINCOLN (1809-1865)

–

No pleasure is comparable to the standing
upon the vantage-ground of truth.

FRANCIS BACON (1561-1626)

–

I searched through rebellion, drugs, diet,
mysticism, religion, intellectualism and
much more, only to find that truth
is basically simple and feels good,
clear and right.

CHICK COREA

–

WISDOM IN HUMILITY

Wisdom means keeping a sense of the fallibility of
all our views and opinions, and of the uncertainty
and instability of the things we most count on.

GERALD BRENAN, FROM "THOUGHTS IN A DRY SEASON"

–

It is the province of knowledge to speak, and it is
the privilege of wisdom to listen.

OLIVER WENDELL HOLMES SR

–

Only the truly wise doubt their wisdom.

PAM BROWN, B.1928

–

It often shows a fine command of language
to say nothing.

FROM "SHARE THE HOPE"

–

The wise say little, think a lot.

PAM BROWN, B.1928

–

Sometimes it proves the highest understanding
not to understand.

BALTASAR GRACIÁN (1601-1658)

–

In seeking wisdom, the first step is silence, the
second listening, the third remembering, the
fourth practicing, the fifth – teaching others.

IBN GABIROL

–

What is wisdom?

For in wisdom there is a spirit intelligent and holy, unique of its kind, made up of many parts, subtle, free-moving, lucid, spotless, clear, invulnerable, loving what is good, eager, unhindered, beneficent, kindly towards others, steadfast, unerring, untouched by care, all-powerful, all-surveying, and permeating all intelligent, pure, and delicate spirits... the man who rises early in search of her will not grow weary in the quest, for he will find her seated at his door.

THE APOCRYPHA
FROM "THE WISDOM OF SOLOMON"

–

Most people fear wisdom.
Simply by existing it devalues power and greed and superficial fame.

PAM BROWN, B.1928

–

Humility, unostentatiousness,
non-injuring, forgiveness,
simplicity, purity,
steadfastness,
self-control; this
is declared to be wisdom.

BOOK OF DAILY
THOUGHTS AND PRAYERS

"THIS TOO WILL PASS"

If I were asked to give what I consider the single
most useful bit of advice for all humanity, it
would be this: Expect trouble as an inevitable part
of life, and when it comes, hold your head high,
look it squarely in the eye and say, "I will be
bigger than you. You cannot defeat me."
Then repeat to yourself the most comforting
of all words, "This too shall pass."

ANN LANDERS, B.1918

—

Truly, it is in the darkness that one finds the light,
so when we are in sorrow,
then this light is nearest of all to us.

MEISTER ECKHART

—

Grief is itself a medicine.

WILLIAM COWPER (1731-1800)

—

A SIMPLER LIFE

How simple and frugal a thing is happiness: a
glass of wine, a roast chestnut, a wretched little
brazier, the sound of the sea....
All that is required to feel that here and now is
happiness is a simple, frugal heart.

NIKOS KAZANTZAKIS (1885-1957)

–

FREEDOM FROM DESIRE LEADS
TO INWARD PEACE.

LAO-TZU (6TH CENTURY B.C.)

–

Ah yet, ere I descend to the grave
May I a small house and a large garden have;
And a few friends, and many books, both true,
Both wise, and both delightful too!

COMTE DE BUSSY-RABUTIN

—

My tip for the twenty-first century? Want less.
Want about half what the Joneses have. If you
want less stuff, you don't need as much money
and then you don't need to work so hard and
then you get time to have fun. Am I making
any sense?

AUTHOR UNKNOWN

—

The ability to simplify means to eliminate the
unnecessary so that the necessary may speak.

HANS HOFMANN

—

A diamond lies about the neck as an anxiety.
A daisy chain as a blessing.

PAM BROWN, B.1928

—

THE WISDOM OF DOING NOTHING

If you can spend a perfectly useless
afternoon in a perfectly useless manner,
you have learned how to live.

LIN YUTANG (1895-1976)

–

Without stirring abroad
one can know the whole world;
Without looking out of the window
one can see the way of heaven.
The further one goes the less one knows.

LAO-TZU (6TH CENTURY B.C.)

–

If you are losing your leisure, look out!
You are losing your soul.

LOGAN PEARSALL SMITH (1865-1946)

–

Work is not always required.... There is such
a thing as sacred idleness, the cultivation of
which is now fearfully neglected.

GEORGE MACDONALD (1824-1905)

—

And men go abroad to admire the heights of
mountains, the mighty billows of the sea,
the long courses of rivers, the vast compass of
the ocean, and the circular motion of the stars,
and yet pass themselves by.

ST. AUGUSTINE (354-430), FROM "CONFESSIONS"

—

Those who [are] unburdened by the past,
undistracted by the future, these are they who
live, who make the best use of their lives; these
are those who have found the secret of
contentment.

ALBAN GOODIER, FROM "THE SCHOOL OF LOVE"

—

ACCEPTANCE

To everything there is a season,
and a time for every purpose
under heaven.

ECCLESIASTES, 3:1

–

Happiness and sorrow are twins,
let them come and go like clouds.

YOGASWAMI (1872-1964)

–

Everyone must row with the oars
he has.

ENGLISH PROVERB

–

*God grant me serenity to accept
the things I cannot change, courage
to change the things I can, and wisdom
to know the difference.*

WILLIAM JAMES (1842-1910)

—

*The miracle is not to fly in the air, or to
walk on the water, but to walk on the earth.*

CHINESE PROVERB

—

*Flow with whatever may happen and let
your mind be free. Stay centered
by acceptance. This is the ultimate.*

CHUANG TSE

THE ART OF LIVING

As soon as you trust yourself,
you will know how to live.

JOHANN WOLFGANG VON GOETHE (1749-1832)

—

To know how to grow old is the master-work
of wisdom, and one of the most difficult chapters
in the great art of living.

HENRI FRÉDÉRIC AMIEL (1821-1881)

—

[Knowledge] is finding out something for oneself
with pain, with joy, with exultancy,
with labor, and with all the little ticking,
breathing moments of our lives, until it is ours
as that only is ours which is rooted
in the structure of our lives.

THOMAS WOLFE (1900-1938)

—

It is necessary
to try to pass one's self always;
this occupation
ought to last as long as life.

QUEEN CHRISTINA OF SWEDEN

–

As long as you live,
keep learning *how* to live.

SENECA (c.4 B.C.- c.65 A.D.)

–

Happiness consists not in having much,
but in being content with little.

MARGUERITE COUNTESS OF BLESSINGTON

–

The secret of happiness is not doing what
one likes to do, but in liking what one
has to do.

SIR JAMES M. BARRIE (1860-1937)

–

ONLY IN QUIETNESS...

Serenity is neither frivolity, nor complacency,
it is the highest knowledge and love, it is the
affirmation of all reality being awake at the
edge of all deeps and abysses.

HERMANN HESSE (1877-1962)

–

Only in quietness can the infinity
of wonder find you.

PAM BROWN, B.1928

–

The mind is never right but when it is at peace
within itself.

SENECA (c.4 B.C.-65 A.D.)

–

*Nothing is so strong
as gentleness; nothing
so gentle as real strength.*

ST. FRANCIS DE SALES (1567-1622)

–

Better than a thousand useless words
is one single word that gives peace.

THE DHAMMAPADA

–

Live in peace yourself and then you can
bring peace to others – a peaceable person
does more good than a learned one.

THOMAS À KEMPIS (1379-1471)

–

The one who smiles rather than rages
is always the stronger.

JAPANESE WISDOM

–

THE WEB OF LIFE

THERE IS NO OTHER DOOR TO KNOWLEDGE
THAN THE DOOR NATURE OPENS;
AND THERE IS NO TRUTH EXCEPT THE TRUTHS
WE DISCOVER IN NATURE.

LUTHER BURBANK

—

Whatever befalls the earth befalls the sons of
the earth. Man does not weave the web of life,
he is merely a strand in it. Whatever he does
to the web he does to himself.

CHIEF SEATTLE (1786-1866)

—

They had what the world has lost: the ancient,
lost reverence and passion for human personality
joined with ancient, lost reverence and passion
for the earth and its web of life. Since before
the Stone Age they have tended that passion
as a central, sacred fire. It should be our long
hope to renew it in us all.

JOHN COLLIER (1928-1971)

—

Remain true to the earth.

FRIEDRICH WILHELM NIETZSCHE
(1844-1900)

—

To see a World
in a Grain of Sand,
And a Heaven
in a Wild Flower....

WILLIAM BLAKE (1757-1827)

—

<u>Fools</u>!

Neither man nor woman can be
worth anything until they have
discovered that they are fools.

WILLIAM LAMB, VISCOUNT MELBOURNE

–

The saddest thing about age is that
one suddenly recognizes that one is
old – and not a whit wiser.

PAM BROWN, B.1928

–

Everyone is a damn fool for at least
five minutes every day; Wisdom
consists of not exceeding the limit.

ELBERT HUBBARD

From the cowardice that shrinks
from new truth, from the laziness
that is content with half-truths,
from the arrogance that thinks it
knows all truth, deliver us.

ANCIENT SCHOLAR

–

If at first you don't succeed,
try again. Then quit. No use being
a damn fool about it.

W.C. FIELDS

THE WISDOM OF LOVE

A loving heart is the truest wisdom.

CHARLES DICKENS

–

Treasure the love you receive above all.
It will survive long after your gold and good
health have vanished.

OG MANDINO

–

We try to give our children everything
– when all they need is love
and certainty.

PAM BROWN, B.1928

–

The supreme happiness of life
is the conviction that we are loved.

VICTOR HUGO (1802-1885)

–

Life is to be fortified by many friendships.
To love and to be loved
is the greatest happiness in existence.

SYDNEY SMITH

–

From success you get lots of things, but not that
great inside thing that love brings you.

SAM GOLDWYN (1882-1974)

–

To laugh often and much; to win the respect of
intelligent people and the affection of children;
to earn the appreciation of honest critics...
to know that even one life has breathed easier
because you have lived.
This is to have succeeded.

RALPH WALDO EMERSON (1803-1882)

–

Sorrow, the Great Teacher

Sorrows are our best educators.
A man can see further through a tear
than a telescope.

LORD BYRON (1788-1824)

–

Too much sunshine makes a desert.
In sorrow we discover things which
really matter;
In sorrow we discover ourselves.

ARAB PROVERB

–

... we may measure our road to wisdom by
the sorrows we have undergone.

BULWER

–

Our real blessings often appear
to us in the shape of pains, losses
and disappointments....

JOSEPH ADDISON (1672-1719)

–

The most perfect peace we can attain
in this miserable life consists rather in meek
and patient suffering, than in exemption
from adversity; and those who have most
learnt to suffer will certainly possess the
greatest share of peace.

THOMAS À KEMPIS (1379-1471)

–

In the depth of winter, I finally learned that
within me there lay an invincible summer.

ALBERT CAMUS (1913-1960)

–

<u>Dare it! Jump in!</u>

There are hazards in anything one does, but there are greater hazards in doing nothing.

SHIRLEY WILLIAMS

–

One doesn't discover new lands without consenting to lose sight of the shore for a very long time.

ANDRÉ GIDE

–

Do not follow where the path may lead. Go, instead, where there is no path and leave a trail.

AUTHOR UNKNOWN

–

When we do the best we can,
we never know what miracle is wrought
in our own life, or in the life of another.

HELEN KELLER (1880-1968)

—

To do anything in this world worth doing,
we must not stand back shivering and
thinking of the cold and danger, but jump
in and scramble through as well as we can.

SYDNEY SMITH

—

Don't be afraid your life will end;
be afraid that it will never begin.

GRACE HANSEN

—

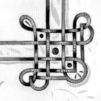

<u>KINDNESS</u>

Kindness is more important than wisdom,
and the recognition of this is the beginning
of wisdom.

THEODORE ISAAC RUBIN

–

They who give have all things;
they who withhold have nothing.

HINDU PROVERB

–

One of the deepest secrets of life
is that all that is really worth doing is what
we do for others.

LEWIS CARROLL (1832-1898)

–

It is one of the most beautiful compensations
of life that no man can sincerely try to help
another without helping himself.

RALPH WALDO EMERSON (1803-1882)

–

*What do we live for, if it is not to make life
less difficult for each other?*

GEORGE ELIOT (MARY ANN EVANS), (1819-1880)

–

Kind words can be short and easy to speak,
but their echoes are endless.

MOTHER TERESA (1910-1997)

–

Everything that is not given is lost.

INDIAN PROVERB

–

Lessons in Courage

Nothing in life is to be feared.
It is only to be understood.

MARIE CURIE (1867-1934)

—

You gain strength, courage, and confidence
by every experience in which you really stop
to look fear in the face. You are able to say to
yourself, "I lived through this horror. I can
take the next thing that comes along."
... You must do the thing you think you
cannot do.

ELEANOR ROOSEVELT (1884-1962)

—

Freedom is full of fear.
But fear isn't the worst thing we face.
Paralysis is.

ERICA JONG, B.1942

Learn from the past.
Do not come to the end of
your life only to find
you have not lived.
For many come to the point of
leaving the space of the earth
and when they gaze back,
they see the joy and the beauty
that could not be theirs
because of the fears they lived.

CLEARWATER

KEEP GROWING...

Always be in a state of becoming.

WALT DISNEY

–

Only in growth, reform and change,
paradoxically enough, is true security to be found.

ANNE MORROW LINDBERGH (1906-2001)

–

I suppose the moments one most enjoys
are moments – alone – when one
unexpectedly stretches something
inside you that needs stretching.

GEORGIA O'KEEFFE (1887-1986)

–

The only real satisfaction there is, is to be
growing up inwardly all the time, becoming
more just, true, generous, simple, manly,
womanly, kind, active.

JAMES FREEMAN CLARKE (1810-1888)

... you must always be displeased by what you are. For where you were pleased with yourself there you have remained. But once you have said, "It is enough," you are lost. Keep adding, keep walking, keep advancing; do not stop, do not turn back, do not turn from the straight road.

ST. AUGUSTINE (354-430)

–

DO NOT FEAR
GOING FORWARD
SLOWLY,
FEAR ONLY
TO STAND STILL.

CHINESE WISDOM

–

What is a *Helen Exley Giftbook?*

Helen Exley has been creating giftbooks for twenty-six years, and her readers have bought forty-one million copies of her works, in over thirty languages. Because her books are all bought as gifts, she spares no expense in making sure that each book is as thoughtful and meaningful a gift as it is possible to create: good to give, good to receive. The themes of personal peace and wisdom are very important in Helen's life, and she has now created several titles on these themes.

Team members help to find thoughtful quotations from literally hundreds of sources, and the books are then personally created. With infinite care, Helen ensures that each illustration matches each quotation, that each spread is individually designed to enhance the feeling of the words, and that the whole book has real depth and meaning.

You have the result in your hands. If you have loved it – tell others! We'd rather put the money into more good books than waste it on advertising when there is no power on earth like the word-of-mouth recommendation of friends.

Helen Exley Giftbooks
16 Chalk Hill, Watford, Herts WD19 4BG, UK
232 Madison Avenue, Suite 1409, New York, NY 10016, USA
www.helenexleygiftbooks.com

Acknowledgements: The publishers are grateful for permission to reproduce copyright material. Whilst every reasonable effort has been made to trace copyright holders, we would be pleased to hear from any not here acknowledged. LAO-TZU: from *Springs of Oriental Wisdom* translated Dr. Peter M. Daly. PAM BROWN: used by permission © 2001.